DEAR ELVIS
Graffiti from Graceland

ELVIS, ITS
1995 AND YOU ARE
STill #1. I CANNOT
EXPLAIN HOW I FEEL WHEN
I HEAR YOU PlAY. I JUST GOTTA
MOVE! TCB
♡ ERIC BILL
Brandy

DEAR ELVIS
Graffiti from Graceland

Daniel Wright

with contributions from Mark Landon Smith

Mustang Publishing Co., Inc.
Memphis, TN • USA

To Sondra, Shana, Nathan, & Callie —
and to Elvis fans everywhere

Library of Congress Cataloging-in-Publication Data
Wright, Daniel, 1967-
   Dear Elvis : graffiti from Graceland / Daniel Wright ; with contributions from Mark Landon Smith.
      p.   cm.
   ISBN 0-914457-75-6
      1. Presley, Elvis, 1935-1977—Homes and haunts. 2. Graceland Mansion (Memphis, Tenn.)
   3. Graffiti—Tennessee—Memphis. I. Smith, Mark Landon. II. Title.
   ML420.P96W75   1996
   782.42166'092—dc20   96-14934
                                                               CIP
                                                               MN

Printed on acid-free paper.
10 9 8 7 6 5 4 3 2 1

Preface

A lot of people have asked how and why I got the idea to write this book. Though I've always been an Elvis fan, my interest never went further than a casual appreciation of the man's music and life.

In the fall of 1989, I had just graduated from college and was about to move away from Memphis to start a job. The night before I left, a friend and I were running around town taking pictures of our favorite sites: Beale Street, the riverfront, Corky's, and of course Graceland. It was the first time in years that I had been to the mansion, and I had forgotten that people routinely wrote their names and left messages and all kinds of graffiti on the wall.

I knew I had to sign the wall before I left Memphis. We ran to a convenience store down the street and bought some markers. As we scrawled our names, I noticed a long, heartfelt poem from "Meagan." It fascinated me. What would inspire someone to put such intimate thoughts, fears, and hopes for all the world to see on the wall of a deceased singer's home? It was funny, touching, and just a little weird. I took a picture of Meagan's poem and forgot about it.

Three years later, when I had reluctantly decided to return to school, my route took me through Memphis, so I made a detour past Graceland. The mansion had become a kind of touchstone for me, a place to reconnect with my home, forget my worries — and usually read some great graffiti. On this particular trip, I was feeling anxious and uncertain about my future, but when I drove up to the wall, the first thing I saw was "Elvis liked his bacon crispy!" in huge letters. It cracked me up. At that time, I knew very little about Elvis's life —and certainly nothing about the man's preference in bacon texture. I just assumed that someone was trying to be funny, and it worked. The goofy graffiti immediately lifted my spirits, and suddenly I saw my future very clearly: I would compile the best graffiti from Graceland's wall into a book and hope that others would find the phenomenon as interesting, amusing, and inspiring as I did.

Since then, I have made innumerable trips to Graceland with notepad in hand. I've spent countless hours transcribing graffiti, and I've met many delightful people. I've discovered that Elvis fans can be as comical as they are sincere, as articulate as they are devoted. And I've learned that the rebellious urges which Elvis aroused over 40 years ago continue to inspire the generations, as I watched both grandmothers and grandsons leave their messages to the King.

Writing this book has been a blast, and I hope you enjoy reading it as much as I enjoyed creating it.

Many people have helped with this project: First, thanks to my parents, Don and Sharra, for the love and support they give their "free spirit" son; to my collaborator and friend Mark Landon Smith for those meteoric coattails I'm riding on; to Randy Holleschau for encouraging me to persevere; to Rollin Riggs at Mustang Publishing for his patience with a novice author; to Robert Gordon for his artful Introduction; to everyone at Elvis Presley Enterprises for cheerful and patient help; to all "The Friends" who encourage liberally, support fanatically, and love regardless; and most of all to God, who put me here and gave me something to say.

Daniel Wright

Foreword

Vernon Chadwick

"Graffiti" is a useful starting point for describing the diverse writings collected in this unique book—at turns funny, heartfelt, visionary, subversive, and apocalyptic—all inscribed on the fieldstone wall that divides Graceland from the cacophony and traffic of Elvis Presley Boulevard. Elvis built this wall and the famous musical gates soon after moving there in 1957. Ironically, the wall and gates that were meant to secure Elvis's privacy soon became a magnet for the 24-hour vigil maintained by legions of fans, some of whose scribblings, like the initials of ancient tourists etched in the pyramids of Gezer, can now be read by all.

While Elvis was alive, but increasingly after his death, visitors to Graceland found the wall a tempting space for a variety of communiqués: personal greetings, jokes, prayers, poems, love letters, votive offerings. What normally would be considered acts of vandalism were in fact acts of devotion by some of the politest and best-intentioned fans in the world. As there is something deeply liberatory about the appropriation of public surfaces for the devious scrawling of personal speech, what better way to pay one's respects to the rock 'n roll rebel than to doodle on his famous wall?

Elvis graffiti, however, is just a fragment of the larger Elvis text, so huge and multi-dimensional that it has become one of the universal texts of the modern world. The word "Elvis" signifies more than any other unit of language in current communication. While this vast field of discourse is still localized in geographical places like Graceland, the Elvis text has broken free of its historical moorings and now lives a life of its own in mass media and global communications. So "graffiti" is only a starting point for grasping the form and function of this universal text of Elvis, this *vox populi* of grace spreading over the land.

At the degree-zero of dream, Elvis is a Universal Ombudsman—comforting, interceding, offering solutions to problems that elude us mere mortals. He is lover, parent, friend, redeemer—a cosmic go-between capable of bringing boy and girl, husband and wife, the living and the dead back together again. Of all the various tones of the graffiti from the wall, it's the passion and fervor that will strike the reader the most. Let's face it: to his ever-expanding, non-denominational following, Elvis is nearly a candidate for sainthood. Every aspect of Elvis's living memory today—from pilgrimages to Graceland to the observance of Elvis Tribute Week to the Candlelight Vigil—parallels similar practices and rituals, including the writing of graffiti, in the history of orthodox religions.

"Dear" is both a salutation of address and a term of endearment, and this book lives up to its title, **Dear Elvis**, beautifully. One can't help but be moved by the intimate, first-name relationship that millions of people have with the King of Rock. Elvis had a God-given ability to communicate with people of all races, cultures, generations, and backgrounds. Call it charisma, showmanship, personality, or magic, its power remains a mystery.

With astonishing blindness, some critics today discount the significance of the enthusiasm for and devotion to Elvis that a sizable portion of humanity enjoys. First, such dismissal is just bad scholarship, since it willfully denies the obvious: Elvis has become a major figure in world history whether you like it or not. No brag, just fact. Second, and more disturbing, their attitudes may be motivated by unfortunate prejudices of class, culture, race, and region, which have no place in today's global community.

Those who free themselves from such prejudices, as Elvis himself did, and open up to his soulful song will begin to understand the central message of the graffiti from Graceland: "It is more blessed to give than to receive." The graffiti collected in this book—poetic fragments from the vast universal text—are moving examples of this truth, a "return to sender" with thanks for all that Elvis has given the world.

Vernon Chadwick is founder and director of the International Conference on Elvis Presley at the University of Mississippi, where he teaches literature, cultural studies, and Elvis. He is the editor of **In Search of Elvis: Music, Race, Art, Religion** *(HarperCollins).*

Contents

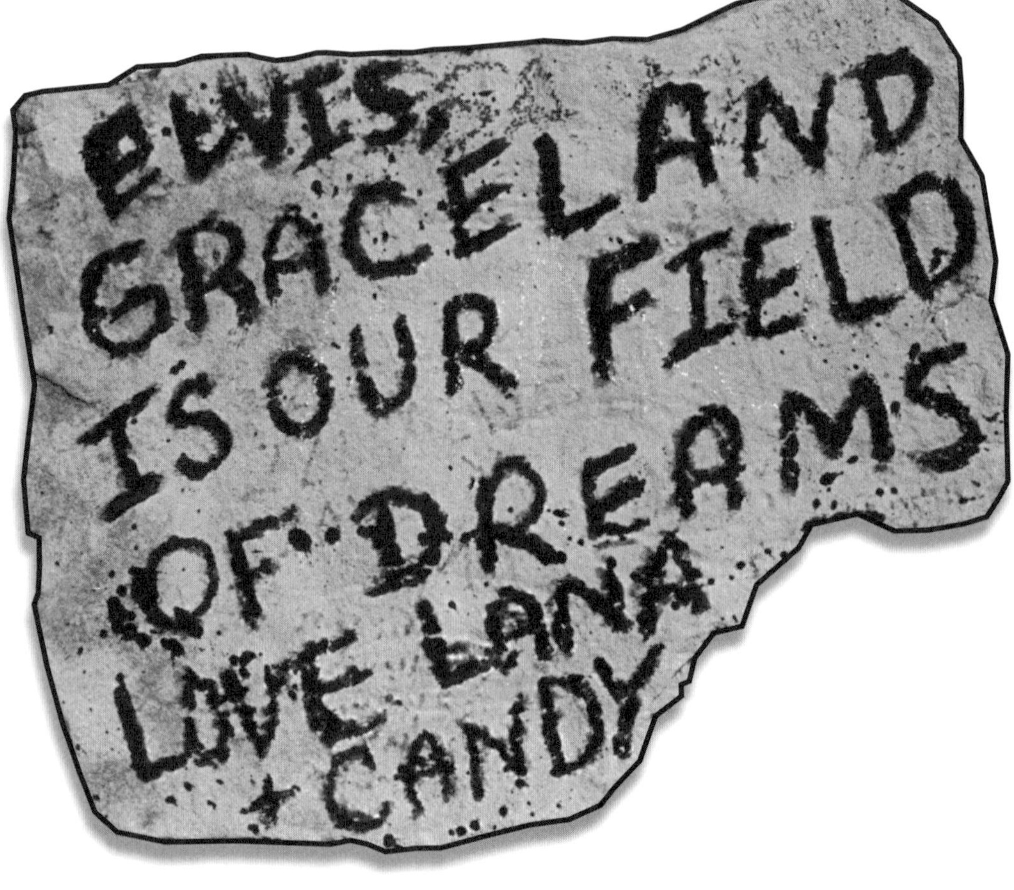
ELVIS,
GRACELAND
IS OUR FIELD
OF DREAMS
LOVE LANA
+ CANDY

Introduction

Robert Gordon

You were there when he was **sipping** a Coke and clowning around and Scotty grinned and looked at the floor. Sam poked his head out the door, and you were there when, it seemed like minutes later, Sam took the acetate of "Blue Moon of Kentucky" to Dewey Phillips and everyone responded with questions, because this was the answer we were waiting for.

You hung out at the donut shop and you spent all your money on the jukebox, because you could swipe donuts but you couldn't swipe plays on the jukebox. You grew sideburns. You screamed in a very high register with the other girls. You got tough, you got loose. You got wild. You found out that aerosol cans made great flamethrowers, and you served a brief term in a detention center for setting old ladies' beehives afire.

"This song is for me," you told your girlfriends, and even though everyone knew you didn't know Elvis, they believed you. But they also believed that the song was for them.

You exchanged ice cream floats for beer, beer for wine, wine for G&T's with lemon on warm afternoons. You played one last game of chicken with your car, let him kiss you, let her kiss you, got married. You raised the kids while he worked. You walked in the front door every afternoon at 5:17 and wished you didn't have to leave each morning. When the kids were screaming, you looked at that door and let your head go through it while your body stayed behind, to the World's

Fair, to Hawaii, to "Love Me Tender." You drank martinis. You thought the Beatles were not as good as sliced bread but better than canned asparagus. You grew a ponytail, braids, hair over your ears, and you put your kids in tie-dye — but taught them to say "ma'am" and "sir." They thought the Beatles were better than toast.

You got promoted. You went back to school. Your kids began to graduate, and now the family had two incomes. You traveled. You sat in a place that was not like home, your kids along this time, and "Blue Moon of Kentucky" came on the radio, and your kids asked about growing up, and you hailed the waiter and ordered a portable phone. When the conversation was done, you hung up and turned to the family and said, "Pack your bags. We're going to Memphis."

"Memphis, Egypt?" asked your youngest, and you knew it was at the prompting of your oldest. Trying to get your goat.

Memphis was hot as hell and the family was grouchy because you regaled them the whole way with boring stories about bobbysox and bobby pins and Bobby Jean. (You know what you didn't tell them about Bobby Jean.) Your cab driver was funny as he drove you to Graceland. "I knew Elvis once," the cabbie said, and there was an audible sigh from everyone, as if this had been prearranged or was under your control. The cabbie said one of Elvis' buddies had hailed him late one night in the 1960's, jumped in and said, "Follow that car!" "And I followed that car. It ran red lights and I ran red lights. It went over the speed limit and I went over the speed limit. About a half-hour later, I pulled up alongside the car and it was Elvis behind the wheel and he was laughing hysterically and everyone in his car laughed and my fare laughed, and there was another car that also had been in the chase and they all laughed. Elvis paid with a hundred-dollar bill, said keep the change, and he signed the bill for me."

You pay the fare with a hundred-dollar bill and the cabbie looks back at you real quick and real hard. You get the change, but you tip him better than usual. Your oldest is the last one out of the car, and he leans back in and asks the cabbie, "Is it true that Elvis wore ladies' underwear monogrammed with his own initials?" The cabbie laughs and sputters on the windshield, and your oldest shakes his hand, grinning wide, and there you are standing across the street from the great mansion.

"It's smaller than I thought it would be," says one of your kids, and your spouse says, because you are kind of choked up, "Yes, but it stands for something awful big."

The Elvis shopping malls sort of bother you, but your kids love it and are much more interested in buying stuff than seeing the house. So you save about a hundred dollars and don't go on the tours, but you spend about a thousand dollars on coffee mugs and postcards and CDs and a dozen other things with Elvis's face on them.

Laden with shopping bags, thirsty, hungry, and very, very hot, you manage to convince the whole family to walk across the street for a closer look at the mansion. The heat from the asphalt makes you all feel woozy, and you think for a minute that maybe the family unit is melting right in front of your eyes. There's a plaque out front and you stop to read it. "Hey, did you know..." you begin to say, but as you turn you see your kids huddled together in a clump beside the long fieldstone wall, and you have that parental feeling of knowing they are doing something wrong, and you are instantly upon them. Caught! You grab the thick markers from their hands and start to berate them for defacing property, especially property that is not theirs to deface, when your spouse approaches and begins to giggle and so do the kids, so you stop because you realize you're the brunt of a joke that you didn't even know existed.

"I gave them the markers," your spouse says, extending a marker toward you. You see that the wall is covered with messages, and though you haven't put graffiti on a wall since you took the grease out of your hair, you take the marker, draw a thin Mona Lisa mustache above your lips, say to your kids, "It's only rock 'n roll," and then you approach the wailing wall and compose your own message to the rebel, writing

DEAR EL,

(you are on a first-syllable basis with Elvis)

DEAR EL, SO IT'S COME TO THIS.

Robert Gordon is the author of **It Came from Memphis** *(Faber & Faber) and the producer of the companion CD (Upstart/Rounder). He also wrote* **The King on the Road** *(St. Martin's), produced the box set of Al Green's music (The Right Stuff/Capitol), and directed the documentary of Beale Street and the blues,* **All Day & All Night**.

Part 1:

OFF THE WALL

If this was Disneyworld, I'd buy a pair of Elvis ears!

ELVIS, I WISH I WAS YOUR BELT BUCKLE FOR A DAY! GINA

Elvis IS in Amway

LUNCH DATE WITH ELVIS BUT HE NEVER SHOWED

Please quit writin' on my wall. Thank you. Thank you very much. "E"

Elvis, we've left the building. — Jeff & Gail

My momma doesn't like your music, but I'm kosher.
— Rima

Elvis, I loved that Jungle Room!
— Jeff

We now know the full power of your shades!

George Burns is bringing cigars and news about Ann-Margret!

ELVIS, YOU WERE IN MY DREAM AND YOU WERE EATING HOT BUTTERED POPCORN.

ELVIS, LEND US SOME MONEY

E, Thanks for carpeting the ceilings of our hearts!

Elvis had A TATTOO Too!

17

Elvis, I will wed on your birthday.
Help me! — Laura

**Yo Elvis! How about getting me
and Muriel together? — Chris**

*Elvis, yesterday I realized how much I love you,
so I broke off my engagement to Adam. Please
come home to Mama! — Monique*

***Elvis, you had great taste in women.
Priscilla is a babe! —Dave***

I KNOW ELVIS

The big men wear long sideburns in memory of Elvis and tasty snack cakes.

If Elvis hadn't been a Rock Star, he would have been a Scientist.
—Joanna

ELVIS KICKS BUTT!

You had A weird Decorator. Thank God He Didn't write music! —Connie

19

Elvis —
Wake up
and go
back to
sleep!

Elvis —
You're all
that and
a bag of
chips!

Mark signed your wall and if you were alive,
you'd be the luckiest king on earth!

Elvis, thanks for helping me celebrate my Fortieth Birthday. Too bad you missed the Party!   Sheila

Elvis, Elvis,
Let me be.
Keep your pelvis
far from me!

Turkey
loves
Elvis! AND VICE-VERSA I BET!

ELVIS=CUTE?

Elvis spoke in class today. He said he loved Pearl!

Elvis, I never believed you were dead, even though the Enquirer said so. For more information, call BR-549. — Jerry

Elvis, I'm bearing your ghost child, and I'm confused because I'm a man!

We love you, and so does the rest of Oz!
— Melissa

You wouldn't have liked the way Caddies look today, anyway.
— Mary Lou

IN THE NAME
OF ELVIS,
I EAT CHEESE

I have met your friend,
I have seen your home,
I have walked your steps,
I will never be the same.

The
President
lives in
Washington,
D.C., but
the King is
from
Memphis!

"If You caN't Find a Partner,
Use a Wooden Chair"?!?
Ouch!

E. — What a long, strange trip
you've been! Dave & Cork

I love shag.
Therefore,
I love Elvis!
— D.J.

Mike — Where
are you in '92?
Like, Elvis
didn't show…

Elvis, no matter where you are,
there you are! — Dave

For reasons I cannot explain there's a part of me that wants to see Graceland...
Jacqueline

Elvis, you're a plush bunny!

Did Elvis start the Hair Club for Men?

E. P. PhONE HoME!

Have a peanut butter sandwich on me, Elvis.
—Cheryl

25

Elvisly yours forever,
Sharon — England

**Nothing better than a cheese steak,
a pint, and Elvis at Cauley's. — Tany**

*Thank you for making my Mom as happy
as Roger has made me! — Tracy*

The only reason Memphis exists: ELVIS!

Elvis, you are the grooviest! UH HUH! Molly

Oh, man, I can hardly believe it!

USA NEEDS AN ELVIS HOLIDAY

Thanksgiving and Elvis are like Apple Pie and America!

Too much, too soon, Elvis.

Elvis, you have your blue suede shoes, but I have my blue python boots.

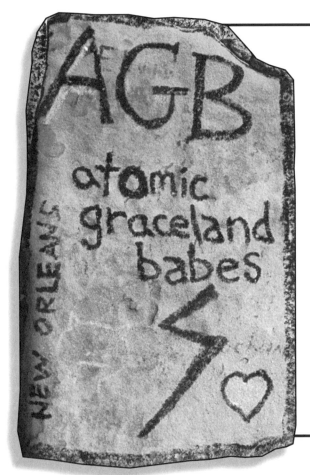

I'll see ya in the
New Order, Elvis!

EARN YOUR 'BURNS!
— JAY

I've been to Mt. Vernon.
I've been to Monticello.
I have to say, though, our
Founding Fathers don't have
anything on Graceland.
Long live the King!

Once a King always a king. But once a Knight is ENOUGH!!!

HE'S THE CUTEST JAILBIRD I EVER DID SEE!

ELVIS, I WANT A SCARF! DIEDRA

I can't believe I'm doing this! Please don't sandblast me!
—Riedy

ELVIS: HOW ABOUT A TENNIS LESSON?

If you're gonna walk the walk, you gotta, like, talk too, or something. — Jen, Barbie, & Paul

King — Loved your pad, but how about some complimentary peanut butter and 'nanner sammiches?

The USA has 41 presidents, but only one King! —TMM

In the great divide between a life with meaning and one without, there is Graceland. — D.B.

ELVIS
says Hi!
MEOW!
Janet

Elvis, You Are the
Sexiest Man I Have
Ever seen! -Jenny

Road Trip '95!
We're here 'cause
We're not all here!
Michelle,
Kelly,
& Nicole

Keep on Rubberneckin'
Elvis!

WITHOUT ELVIS YOU ARE NOTHING!
HE OWES NOBODY!- MIDGE

31

Elvis, you sang a song for me, so I'm gonna sing one for you! Dewayne

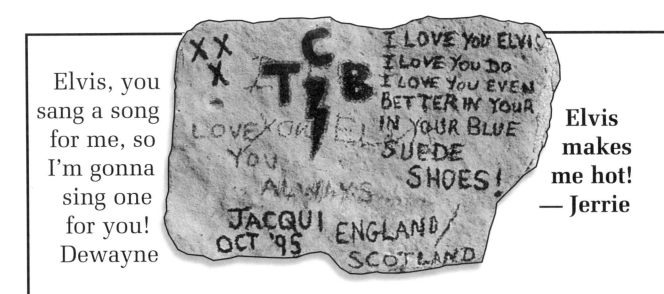

Elvis makes me hot! — Jerrie

Elvis, you could sing "Mary Had a Little Lamb" and it would become a hit. Thanks for sharing your talent with the world.

GET THE
GOAT, GET
THE PRIZE!

JUDY IS ELVIS'S
LOVE cHILD!

I made it! My life is
complete! All my love
forever, Dianne

The King Lives!
(No! Really! He does!)

Elvis and Nixon-
TogeTher Again!

TOO MUCH SOUL
TO CONTROL!
MARTHA

ELVILicious!

33

Elvis, you are one handsome hound dog!
—Anna

**ELVIS, YOU WILL ALWAYS
RULE MEMPHIS! —BELINDA**

*Elvis, you made us all so very happy! Thank you
for being you. But we want you to be happy, too!*

***Maynard loved music,
and so do I!***

IF ONE MAN loves ANOTHER MAN,
THEN ONE MAN MUST be elvis.
— Les

I preferred
the Beatles

ELVIS
HEALS

Elvis, I Lust
you hard.
—Cammi

DEAR GLADYS & VERNON—YOU DONE GOOD!

The Graceland Experience

Graceland. It's a lovely word, conjuring thoughts of serenity, hospitality, and elegance. The charming name of Elvis Presley's mansion, however, can evoke many different reactions.

To Elvis, Graceland meant one thing: home. Throughout his adult life, he placed enormous value on his 13.8-acre estate in south Memphis. Graceland was where Elvis could relax with his family and friends after weeks of performing around the country, besieged by fans and the media. The privacy and peace he found behind the famous musical gates were priceless to him.

To fans, Graceland symbolizes a precious memorial, a place to honor the myriad achievements of Elvis Presley — the performer, the philanthropist, and the man who came from the humblest of beginnings to achieve worldwide fame and respect.

To Elvis's detractors, Graceland is shorthand for a silly circus, a place that appeases tourists visiting the shrine and collecting the souvenirs of a pop-culture curiosity.

Those who are neither ardent fans nor critics find Graceland an enigma, a place where, for some reason, people seem compelled to gather. While a few of those people confirm the stereotypes — polyester jumpsuits, beehive hairdos, trailer-park twangs — most visitors to Elvis's home represent as broad a cross section of humanity as you could imagine. The evidence? Their messages on the wall, which prove they come from all over the world and all walks of life: cashiers and lawyers, waitresses and doctors, college students, newlyweds, and grandparents. They live in Boston, Birmingham, Berlin, and Bangkok. Some were dragged to Memphis by enthusiastic partners; others hocked an heirloom for gas money to get to rock music's Mecca.

Despite the huge variety of visitors to the mansion, there are two common denominators. Each of them, in some way large or small, was touched by the life of Elvis Presley. And almost every person who visits Graceland will write something on the wall.

A Little History

The land on which Graceland now stands had been a farm from Civil War times to the mid-1930's. In 1939, Dr. and Mrs. Thomas Moore built a Georgian mansion on the property, which was named for Mrs. Moore's great-aunt, Grace Toof. The Moores considered the estate their "country home" —the city of Memphis was still miles away in those days — and they raised a musically talented daughter, Ruth Marie, there.

In 1957, the house, which had been the temporary home of Graceland Christian Church, was listed for sale and shown to Gladys and Vernon Presley by a real estate agent named Virginia Grant. Though the Presleys were comfortable in their home at 1034 Audubon Drive, they were overwhelmed there by fans at all hours, and their neighbors were getting annoyed. Elvis's parents loved Graceland and were anxious to show it their son, who was in Hollywood filming *Loving You.* When Elvis toured the estate, he knew he could create a refuge there from the increasingly insatiable press and public.

On March 7, 1957, Elvis purchased Graceland for $102,500. He paid $40,000 in cash, used $25,500 from the sale of the house on Audubon, and got a mortgage for $37,000 with Equitable Life at 4% interest. Only 22 years old, he had bought a dream home for his family. Just look how far they had come from Lauderdale Courts, the dreary public housing complex where they had lived just four years earlier! Elvis planned to turn part of the acreage back into a working farm so his mother could raise chickens.

Graceland and Graffiti

Graceland today is considerably different from the home Elvis purchased in 1957. Throughout the 20 years he lived there, Elvis constantly renovated, adding recreation facilities, a chicken coop, a trophy room, the Meditation Garden, and garages. Two of his first touches were installing the renowned musical gates and the long wall of Alabama fieldstone, on which fans quickly began writing messages.

While Elvis was alive, the groundskeepers did their best to keep the wall clean. After his death, however, the sheer volume of the graffiti proved overwhelming, and officials with the estate decided to leave the wall alone. Occasionally, somebody will write something crude or irrelevant, and Graceland hires a firm that uses high-pressure water equipment to clean the wall. Contrary to rumor, however, Graceland does not periodically sandblast the wall. It's the weather that does the damage to the graffiti; the sun and rain fade most messages within a year.

Today, writing on the wall is as much a part of the Graceland experience as seeing the Jungle Room and the grave

Walter Branch washes off graffiti expressing support for a high school football team.

site. The wall is so long that you could spend hours reading from one end to the other. As you read, you'll likely see several tourists with markers in hand stopping to add their messages or have their snapshots taken next to a memorable piece of graffiti. Celebrities in town for a film or concert often pay tribute on the wall. One publicized incident involved rocker Billy Idol, who painted "Long live the King" in huge red letters.

Most messages are sincere and polite: people write their names, hometowns, and a brief endearment like "We love and miss you, Elvis!" When the rare vulgarity or negative comment does appear, it doesn't last long — an Elvis fan will come along shortly and cover it up.

Though some graffiti defies description, most can be placed into one of the three categories in this book. Some people are deliberately wacky and clever, and

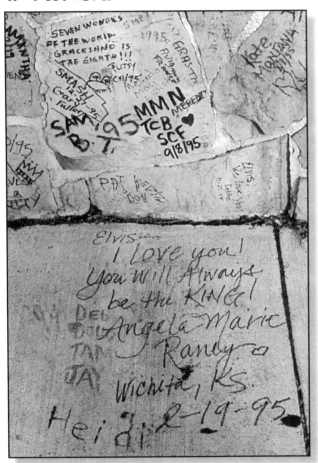

some are convinced Elvis is alive and are looking for him. But the most memorable messages are from people whose lives were affected by the man's unparalleled musical gifts, which he generously shared with the world for 25 years. His songs, his voice, and the story of his life — the quintessential legend of a "poor boy made good" — inspire the bulk of the graffiti on that long fieldstone wall. The grammar is occasionally poor, the spelling is often bad, and the markers are sometimes almost out of ink, but the honesty and love are always legible.

The very act of writing graffiti is one of rebellion, and many people are surprised at the lack of crudeness and hostility along the wall. But that's what Elvis fans have in common with the man who called Graceland home: they know how to rebel with style.

When there's no room left on the wall, fans write on the sidewalk.

Part 2:

WANTED: ELVIS

Elvis— Meet me at the K-Mart (in lingerie)! Jenny

HEY ELVIS, ARE YOU LONESOME TONIGHT? -Rachelle

My dear sweet love Elvis. You are all I have. -Val

They needed a little "soul" in heaven. You are gone but not forgotten. We love you! Shannon

Elvis, are you in there? Come out,
come out wherever you are!

**Elvis, until I see you on that beautiful
shore, I miss and love you! —Phyllis**

*Elvis is alive and works security
at Northside Mall in Slidell, LA.*

***From Massachusetts, with love.
If you're alive, please call me soon.
—Dale***

ELVIS, Wake 'em up in heaven!

1-800-1 SAW ELVIS

Elvis, it's me again in '93. Remember?

I wasn't much of a fan before, but somehow you hit something inside. I never knew you had the magic, but you got me... I believe in the King!

HEY BABY! I HATE TO ASK, BUT I HAVE A SUSPICIOUS MIND-- ARE YOU ALIVE? ANDY

10-6-95
Without So a song a man
caint got a friend.
Without a song, the
road would never bend.
Without a song the day
Would never end.
So Elvis keep singing
your Song! Stacey + Steph

Elvis, you are still
my man! — Rose

**Elvis: I pray you
are alive and well!
— Larry**

*Nice meeting you, Elvis!
— The Lara Family*

***Elvis is here...
With the truth!***

As long as we keep Elvis on our minds, there is a promised land for the future. Angela

Hey ELViS: Lisa Marie Made a big Mistake! Come back and Straighten Her Out! Mary, 1994

ELVIS THANKS FOR DRIVING US TO YOUR HOME! YOU THROW A HELLUVA PARTY

You came to us, a poor boy from Tupelo, and you gave us ALL you had! You rocked the WORLd!! You will always be the KING! A legend of aLL time! You ARE the greatest!!!

45

My body lies, but I still roam.

**Elvis, you can come back out now.
We know why you left.**

*Elvis was an angel sent from heaven. He did his job
and God took him from us, but he will always live.*
                                    —Julie

You're still the best part of my heart.
                        —Tina, Finland

DEAR GOD: BOLTON AND CYRUS FOR PRESLEY?!?

LET'S TRADE!!!

Elvis is **NOT** dead! He lives on the second floor! – Rick

ELVIS, Get Well SOON! Love, Brett, Heather, Leah, and Ritchie

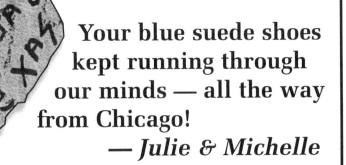

ELVIS you will always be the KING of MUSIC Carlsbad Texas 18-93 TCB

Your blue suede shoes kept running through our minds — all the way from Chicago!
— *Julie & Michelle*

Came from Brooklyn, NY. You helped make this the best birthday! It was worth the trip! — *Jennifer*

Thank you for helping us believe in our dreams!
Robert & Janice, married 8/16/92 in Memphis

ELVIS, IF YOU ARE ALIVE, WILL YOU PLAY KARDINEA PARK ON YOUR '93 TOUR???

Elvis, my husband Mac wanted to come with me, but now he's in heaven with you. — Love, Flo

Precious Elvis, Life isn't the same without you. Until we meet again, I'll listen to your music and just PRETEND —Annette

While on earth, you were the King of Rock 'N Roll. You sang for all people. Now you sing for the King of all Kings! — Bonnie

Elvis, live long and prosper!
—Jerry

**Elvis, if you were here,
you would be mine! —Nelda**

*Dave and Tina spent their
honeymoon with the King!*

***Dear King, You
invited us, so we came.***

ELVIS DIDN'T DIE! HE MOVED TO A BETTER PLACE!

We've waited for 15 years. If you don't come back before the postage stamp, we know you never will.

ELVIS — JUST STOPPED BY TO SAY HI. GUESS YOU AREN'T IN.
SCOTT & PAM, CANADA

Elvis, Please show Jackie O. a good time!
Chris

Elvis lives, and so does my love for him!
— Cheryl

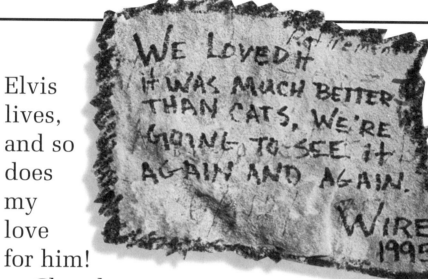

Hey Elvis, Let's ride!

I wish I could've met the King!

We want you, we need you, we love you. Forever.

ELVIS, HOPE YOU'RE
IN HEAVEN. LOVED
YA, BABY!
SONYA

Elvis, you're the greatest star in the
heavens! Along with Patsy, Roy, Buddy,
Dale, Bobby, and Jackie.
If there's a rock-n-roll heaven,
we know it's got a helluva band!
Nancy & Woody

CAN ELVIS COME OUT AND
PLAY?? JEWELS

Elvis makes Life
worth living!
Richie

Elvis, you are an angel.
Literally.

Elvis lives! (Spotted in Blue Springs)

Elvis is alive — and pissed!

From a kid to an old man,
I will remember. — Paolo

TCB with your help and understanding,
I came home today! I love you immensely!
—Dianne

If I can Dream, Elvis **LIVES FOREVER!** Deirdra

Elvis, i came to see you. Come see Me in Michigan. —Kathi

Maybe not in flesh, but your spirit still lives in these walls.

Elvis, please call Kevin. He heard you were dead and he's **BUMMED.**

lay your head on my pillow. lay your warm and tender body next to mine —valerie

I saw Elvis at Denny's!

Elvis, please stand by me.

Elvis-meister, live on! —Stephanie

***Even though I am without
you, you will always be
my hunka hunka
burnin' love! Love
me tender, Amy***

Elvis is in **THAT** house!

Elvis, maybe you're gone, I don't know. But you'll always be the King of rock-n-roll. As you said, "I'll be back." Hope to meet you someday. — Vince

Elvis, I wasn't here when you left, but I'll be here when you come back. Angel

ELVIS ROCKS OUR WORLD! DEE + DORI

ALOHA FROM ISRAEL

Elvis, I hope I'll see you in Heaven.
— Misty

I wish I could walk a mile in your shoes.
— Mark

Elvis, you're still an inspiration. I only
wish I'd had the chance to see you perform.

He touched me and now I am
no longer the same. — Jessica

ELVIS — I'm sixteen years too late, but I'll wait in line 'till I have front row seats in heaven. My love forever! — Jeri

Elvis, you still give us "nguvud na roho" — strength of heart. Magic Elvis Club, Kenya

Elvis, you drive me crazy when I hear your music! Miss you! — Liane, Germany

You never made it To England, but I made iT to You! Louise

I have seen the light. Thank you, Elvis.

Elvis —You're #1 in Canada!
Marge & Lew

Elvis: It's hard growing old without you around. —Deanna

You good-lookin' doll!

DEAR ELVIS
VIVA! SEGUIN TX.
WE'VE COME TO MECCA
TO PAY HOMAGE. WE LOVE
YOU MORE TODAY THAN
YESTERDAY !!!
FOREVER YOURS,
LOVE ALWAYS,
JUDY AND JOAN (THE TWINS)
FOR FELISA'S DAUGHTER, ELVIS... YOU TOO ♡

THERE IS ONLY
ONE KING, AND WE
KNOW WHO HE IS!
HERMAN, YOLANDA,
BETO, IMELDA
AND ALEX
FROM MEXICO!

You don't have to wear a
crown to be a King!
Sven & Kristen, Holland

Elvis, you are the best for us forever!
Your Swiss fans—Pamela, Patrick, & Wolfgang

This was a place for you; now,
a place for us. We miss you!

—Cindy

E, I'm still waiting for my one
night with you! Love you forever!
—Linda

Graceland Trivia

Graceland opened for public tours on June 7, 1982. In the Memphis newspaper the next day, a visitor from Wisconsin was quoted as saying, "I predict this will be closed in two years. The tourists will kill it — they'll steal everything in sight." Today, Graceland receives over 700,000 visitors a year and is considered the most famous home in America — after the White House.

Before Graceland opened for public tours, the trustees of Elvis's estate had received inquiries from the city of Memphis and others about selling the home. Security and maintenance of the mansion were costing the estate hundreds of thousands of dollars a year, and the financial constraints were severe. One price that emerged: $12 million. However, Priscilla Presley enlisted the aid of a stock broker in Kansas City named Jack Soden, and he devised plans to make Graceland the tourist Mecca it is today — and to keep the mansion in the Presley family.

Elvis at home, circa 1957.

Elvis was six years old and living in Tupelo, Mississippi when a large article in the Memphis *Commercial Appeal* on October 27, 1940 described Graceland as "one of the most outstanding homes in Memphis." To an Elvis fan today, the story's quote from owner Ruth Moore is almost eerie:

"'Our entire home is centered around music... The rooms have been designed for future musicales, and space was essential not only for seating purposes but for tone volume.'"

Though fans consider any time at Graceland special, there are three extra-special events each year:

The Holiday Season: Graceland glows with the original Christmas decorations and lights that Elvis used.

Elvis's Birthday: There are always special events and activities for several days around January 8 each year.

Elvis Week: In mid-August each year, Graceland hosts thousands of visitors from around the world to enjoy a full week of memorials, seminars, fan club meetings, and numerous fun events. Elvis Week culminates in the touching Candlelight Vigil, held August 15.

Fans wait beside Graceland's wall for the annual Candlelight Vigil to begin.

Some people say that the ghost of Elvis's mother Gladys still roams Graceland. Elvis himself claimed to have heard her call his name on more than one occasion after her death in 1958.

Amazing Elvis statistics:

☞ Over one billion Elvis records have been sold worldwide — more than any other individual or group in the history of recorded voice.

✎ Elvis had 18 #1 songs and over 90 albums in the top 100. He received 14 Grammy nominations and won four: three for gospel songs and a Lifetime Achievement Award.

✐ Ed Sullivan paid Elvis $50,000 for his three appearances on *The Ed Sullivan Show* in the late 1950's. It was a record sum at the time.

•❖ Elvis made 31 Hollywood films and two concert documentaries.

❧ There are over 500 active Elvis Presley fan clubs around the world.

Delta Mae Presley Biggs, Elvis's aunt, was the last relative of Elvis to live at Graceland. She lived there with her dog Edmund until her death on July 29, 1993 —11 years after public tours of the home began.

Elvis had the Meditation Garden built in the mid-1960's, and he often enjoyed serene moments there. Though he never expressed a desire to be buried at Graceland, his body was moved there in October, 1977 because the security concerns at his grave site had overwhelmed the staff at Forest Hill Cemetery. Gladys Presley's body was moved at the same time.

When Vernon Presley passed away in 1979, he was interred between Gladys and Elvis. In 1980, Elvis's grandmother Minnie Mae was buried next to her grandson. The Garden also holds a memorial to Elvis's twin Jessie Garon, who died at birth and is buried in Tupelo, Mississippi.

Most mornings, Graceland opens its gates for people who want to visit the Meditation Garden. The 90-minute visitation period is free and ends 30 minutes before the day's tours begin.

Part 3:

WITH ALL MY HEART

Elvis, your biggest treasure is the fans who keep in touch on this wall. See ya, Bill

MY HEART STOPPED ON 8-16-77. I LOVE YOU. – EILEEN

THE REASON:

Those who aren't Elvis Fans will never understand the Reason to bE here. We, who Love Him, can't explain it.

A visit to Graceland came true today!
You are the greatest! — Margie

**I'm a true blue fan — I made
the trek to Graceland! — Tom**

*It took 33 years, but I finally made it.
Thanks for keeping me young. — Brett*

***I left my tears at Graceland.
Love you tenderly, Laura***

ELVIS—THANKS FOR GRACELAND. YOU STILL IMPRESS ME WAY TOO MUCH!

Elvis went where others feared to tread. And aren't we glad he did?
—Candy

January 1993: Happy 58th! I was only a child when you died, but I have Learned to love You. I WISH YOU WERE STILL HERE. You are always on my Mind, Always in my heart. You will Live FOREVER. —Donna

MY BOY, MY BOY

ELVIS, YOU TEAR THE STARS FROM OUR SKY.

ELVIS
I CAME
I SAW
I WEPT
TRUELY MOVED
CARRIE

Elvis, I have loved you
since 1956! — Esther

**When stars fall, the
world sings the blues.**

*I made it El! I miss you!
I love you always!*
— E.L.

***Elvis, I'm sorry I was born late.
I love you anyway. — Eva***

Elvis, my wish came true when I heard you sing.
Then one day, you passed away. There was nothing I could say.
I stood there and cried as they carried your body away.
But that was yesterday. Sixteen years ago today.
I loved you then, and I love you now.
I forgot to remember to forget you... Love, Renee

SLEEP WELL,
SWEETHEART.
THEN FLY, SOAR,
WHOOP UP A HOOPIN'!
I'M SORRY THINGS
HURT SO MUCH.
— HAL

E is FOR EveRybody aNd
EveRything that's ELVIS!
— MINDY

ELViS — As an EnTeRtainer, one of a
KIND. As a Man, one oF The kindest.

My husband brought me here
for my memories of you.

**Elvis, I'm taking good care
of your biggest fan. — Lobo**

*Thank you for bringing me
together with the one I love.*

***Rob + Melanie — One year later!
Thanks Elvis!***

I HAD REASON
TO BELIEVE AND
I WAS RECEIVED
AT GRACELAND.
...JANE

Elvis, your amazing talent and uniqueness brought happiness to the lives of millions. Your legacy continues. You will live in our hearts forever. May you rest in peace.   Karen

Thanks, Elvis, for giving some GRACE to the LAND. —Connie

thank you elvis for prayers answered

WHEREVER YOU ARE, ELVIS IS . . .

Elvis, thank you for letting us honor your life.
The King lives on in our hearts! — Katie

Elvis, I have grown to love you because of my Mom. — Michelle

You renew old, lost dreams. Thank you, Elvis. — Chad

I will be true, no matter what they say.

I will be true, though you are far away.

Each night I pray, all day I say

silent prayers that when I open my eyes, I'll find you there.

Somehow I feel that someday we will meet again.

Don't ask me how — it's something I can't explain.

Until the day I give up all hope of you,

assure yourself this I'll do...

I will be true. —Kelly

YOUR SMILE MELTS MY HEART! —VICKI

ELVIS, YOUR BURNING LOVE LEFT A HOLE IN MY HEART!

73

You are the King and you will never die in my heart! — Jason

Elvis, King of my heart!
Love, Eleanor

You'll always be alive in my heart and soul. — Lee

Only the good die young!
— Paulette and Debbie

Elvis — We laughed and we sang and we will never be the same.
— Susan

Elvis, We wish we could have loved you tender enough to keep you with us.
Love — Robert, Carla, & Justin

ELVIS, YOU WERE THE FIRST, THE BIGGEST, AND THE BEST!
ROb

E-TERNAL!

In memory of our Mom & Dad, Joseph & Lucille. Our house was filled with your music.

We're rockin' in your
honor, Blue Suede.

**Elvis, it was you who
changed music forever.**

*Elvis, you
were a good
person.*

*Elvis,
thanks for
the laughter.*

A MESSAGE I WISH TO SHARE WITH MY FRIENDS ELVIS HAS GIVEN ME MORE THAN ANY SOUL CAN GIVE. REACH OUT AND HE WILL BE THERE.

Elvis, I came for a short visit, but a part of me will always remain... Jen

Memphis, where Wishes really do come True. You've goT a prayer in Memphis!
— Colleen

Softly as I leave you,
you're where the angels are.
Softly as I leave you,
always know you are loved.
Softly as I leave you,
we rejoice as your fans.
for softly as I leave you,
you're now in Jesus' hands.——Dana

Elvis, you will always be in my heart.
— Dagmar (Germany)

The King of Rock is a legend Down Under.
From Melbourne, Australia

I love you, Elvis!
I'll see you when I get there.

Elvis — Not to be taken away.

Let's be friends with Elvis! —Germany

I know you have found peace in the valley. Rest in peace.

Elvis we love you so much that we named our little boy Chadwik after you in Blue Hawaii. We miss you! Kathy

elvis: america's answer to royalty. rebecca & jordan

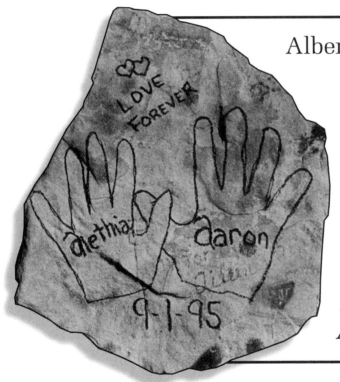

Alberta, Canada misses you!

**We love you!
The Girls from Oklahoma**

*To Elvis, with love from
the U.K. — Paul & Jaquie*

***A tribute to Elvis from
Alberto & Bologna, Italy!***

The music lives on. Elvis is gorgeous! Love you, Vicki

Dear E—"For there are brighter sides to Life. And I should know because I've seen them, but not very often."

Elvis, I waited 13 years to get here. I will Live my whole LiFe through loving You.

DAD, YOU ARE NOW IN HEAVEN WITH THE KING OF ROCK-N-ROLL! THIS IS A MEMORY I WON'T FORGET. YOU AND ELVIS WILL STAY IN MY HEART AND MIND FOREVER.
     LOVE, DEBBIE

ELVIS IS TRUE. He is the King of Rock-n-Roll. There is only one King, and I'm sure that he is having fun with his mother and father in Heaven.

81

We believed before. Now we believe
even more! — Lise & Char

**Elvis, 5 years later, and
it's only stronger. — Steve**

*Elvis, when you get ready, you can
TCB with us! — Sylvia & Skeeter*

***Elvis, what now, my love?
— Kathy***

THE DAYS MAY BE CROWDED, THE HOURS TOO FEW, BUT THERE IS ALWAYS TIME FOR YOU. — LES

ELVIS — WE CAME, WE CONVERSED, AND NOW WE LOVE YOU EVEN MORE! SAM & LAURA

Those things that you hold dear to your heart shall never die.

I'll Remember you. Your voice is as soft AS a warm summer breeze! We Miss You!

ELVIS, I love YOU FOR 100,000 REASONS, BUT MOST OF All I LOVE YOU BECAUSE YOU'RE YOU.

Elvis, you're not my first love, but you are my last.
— Elissa

Elvis, our cups that you filled with joy are now filled with sorrow. We are blind without your light. We understand the truth.

Elvis, I need you/ love you so much every day! Yours always, V.B.

Elvis — One man's life touches so many others'! We love you. —Tim & Kim

THANK YOU dear ELvis for all the happiness and the miracle. Wish I could stay FOREVER. I WiLL Come Back... Hatice

ELViS, I came HERE A Non-believer, BUT I AM leaving here A FAN. You truly are the KiNG. —Hannah

Look up at the sky at midnight. Gaze upon the stars that shine. Just as Heaven knows no boundaries, neither DO MY LOVE AND loyalty to you. You'll be the King of music Forever. Love, Mark

Thank you, Elvis, for your love,
your song, and your soul. — Pate

**Elvis, I know what "always
on my mind" meant. — Leigh**

*Words are not enough to express my
love and respect for you.*

***Elvis — A generation's love, always.
Cindy & Sheila***

HE IS NOW LEADING THE ANGELIC CHOIR IN SWEET INFINITY.

True fans STAY TRUE. Say "HI" to DAD FOR ME. You're BOTH in my HEART. LOVE, D.L.

Standing here, my words fail me. Knowing that you played in This yard makes me Happy. Knowing that you Saw the Same Trees fills me up!

Elvis, this is for the ones who could not be here to share this moment. Thanks for so many happy memories.
— Maria & Mark

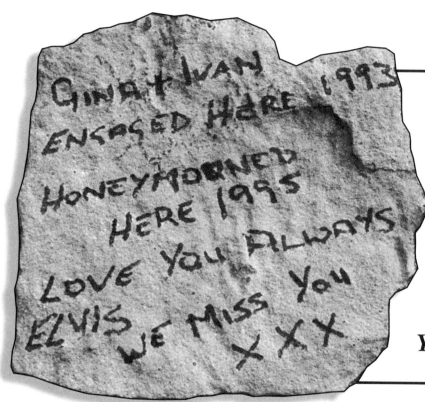

From Tupelo to Tennessee, you stole our hearts and filled our dreams. You'll always be the King to us, Elvis Presley! You're #1!

You are fantastic! I never got to see you, but I have come to Graceland each August for 15 years. It still hurts, but the love from your fans all over this world helps mend these broken hearts. Thank you, Love, for your music and all the wonderful things you did and will forever do. You bring the world together in friendship and love. The world is full of beautiful people. Elvis, you are the most beautiful in every way. The world has learned, and always will learn, much from you and be grateful always. Till next year. You sing forever in our hearts.

ELViS, ThANKS FoR tHE COMFoRT. Stephanie

Now That I'VE been to Graceland And seen it, I have THe UTmost RESPeCT For YOU. KeeP rockin'! — Ben

It was 16 years ago. I was 7, now 23.
Still love you, Elvis. — Shannon

You are so good, kind, and beautiful!
Man, I love you! — Carol

I love you now and forever. I will be
with you someday. I will dream of you
until then. — Jen

I wasn't old enough to know what a loss it was
when you left us, but the memories you have
given us will outlast a lifetime. — Leigh

We traveled a long way, but for YOU we'd do it again in a minute!
T.L.C.!

ELVIS is in my soul! You don't like it? I'LL tell you this, you ain't no fan of the King!

Fifteen years and I still feel the tears. You gave us happiness and love. For that I came to say thank you, my friend!
— Glen

Elvis you touched many people with your gift. Now I know why. Thank you, Teresa

JUST, BECAUSE...
Jacqueline & Eric
The Netherlands

Knowing that your door is always open and your path is free to walk keeps you gentle on my mind. — Keri

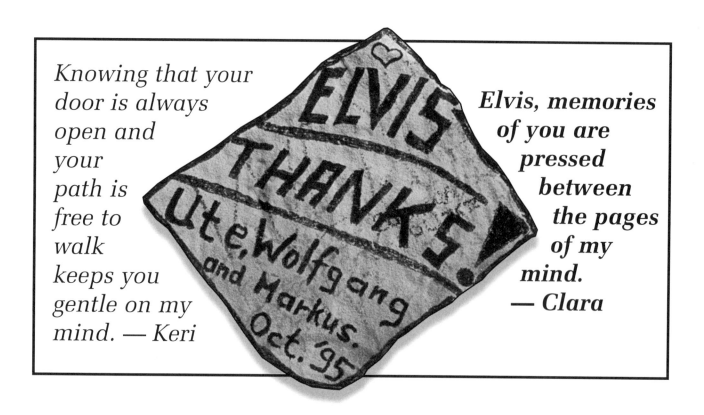

Elvis, memories of you are pressed between the pages of my mind. — Clara

I will embrace him with poetic hands with which to express himself. I will make his voice of cherished velvet, and when he speaks and sings untold beauty and joy will be felt around the world. I will bring his form into the world to bring people together. I will give him riches and love beyond imagination. I will make him unique and irreplaceable in a world of duplication. I will present him to the world as a gift of God, and he will be called **ELVIS PRESLEY.**

93

HAVE YOU SEEN GOOD GRAFFITI AT GRACELAND?
If so, please share it with me for a sequel to this book!
If I use your contribution, I'll send you a free copy of the sequel.
Write to Daniel Wright, c/o Mustang Publishing Co.,
P.O. Box 3004, Memphis, TN 38173 USA

*(**Note:** We welcome your photos, but they cannot be returned and will become the property of Mustang Publishing.)*

More Great Books from Mustang Publishing

The Complete Book of Golf Games by Scott Johnston. Want to spice up your next round of 18 holes? With over 80 great betting games, side wagers, and tournament formats, this book will delight both weekend hackers and the totally obsessed. From descriptions of favorite games like Nassau and String to details on unusual contests like String and Bingo Bango Bongo, it's essential equipment in every golfer's bag. *"A must acquisition."* — *Petersen's Golfing.* **$9.95**

How to Be a Way Cool Grandfather by Verne Steen. There are some things a grandfather just **ought** to know: how to make slingshot from an old limb and a rubber band, how to make a kite from a newspaper, how to do a few simple magic tricks, and how to make his grandkids say, "Cool, Grandpa!" This is a great book for every old fogey who'd rather be way cool. **$12.95**

Europe for Free by Brian Butler. If you're traveling on a tight budget — or if you just love a bargain — this book is for you! With thousands of things to do and see for free all over Europe, you'll save lots of lira, francs, and pfennigs. *"Well-organized and packed with ideas."* — *Modern Maturity.* **$9.95**

Also in this series:
London for Free ($8.95) • **DC for Free ($8.95)** • **Hawaii for Free ($8.95)** • **Paris for Free (Or Extremely Cheap) ($8.95)** • **The Southwest for Free ($8.95)**

ે ે ે

Mustang books should be available at your local bookstore. If not, send a check or money order for the price of the book, plus $2.00 postage **per book**, to Mustang Publishing, P.O. Box 3004, Memphis, TN 38173 U.S.A. To order by credit card, call toll free 800-250-8713 (or 901-521-1406). Allow three weeks for delivery. For rush, one-week delivery, add $2.00 to the total. **International orders:** Please pay in U.S. funds, and add $5.00 to the total for Air Mail.

For a complete catalog of Mustang books, send $1.00 and a stamped, self-addressed, business-size envelope to Catalog Request, Mustang Publishing, P.O. Box 3004, Memphis, TN 38173 U.S.A.